And God Said . . . Just Walk

And God Said . . . Just Walk

Written by Karen D. Spencer
(Inspired by God)

VANTAGE PRESS
New York

Cover design by Susan Thomas

FIRST EDITION

Published by Vantage Press, Inc.
419 Park Ave. South, New York, NY 10016

Manufactured in the United States of America
ISBN: 0-533-15424-3

Library of Congress Catalog Card No.: 2005910919

0 9 8 7 6 5 4 3 2 1

Contents

Preface

I want to begin by thanking my Father, Jesus Christ, my Lord and Savior. If not for Him I would not be writing this book. I want to make it clear that this book was written as a direct order from God the Father. He has given me the information as to what is to be placed in His book as well as all the titles for the chapters. I take no credit for anything. I am merely a vessel for the Lord doing His will, as I was instructed.

In a course of twenty-one years a lot has occurred. It's funny how time seems to pass slowly, yet in a blink of an eye time travels faster than the speed of lightning. This book spans over the course of my life, ranging from the age of seven when the Lord first spoke to me and ending with the Lord healing my body and instructing me on how to spread the news that He is here. Sit back, relax, and get ready to receive the precious gifts the Lord has to offer you.

Acknowledgments

I would like to begin by giving all honor, praise, and glory to Jesus

Christ my Lord and Savior who is the center of my life. Amen.

I would like to give honor to Bishop and Mrs. James A. Johnson for the outstanding work Bishop does in delivering the Word of God. Bishop, you are a fine shepherd of your flock of sheep. I would also like to honor my first assistant pastor Elder and Sister William and Evelyn Bryant, and my second assistant pastor Elder Walter and Evangelist Barbara Cole.

I would like to thank my uncle and aunt, Bishop Roland E. Hairston, Psy.D and Minister June Hairston, D.D. for their words of encouragement and for their belief in me. I love you both.

I would like to thank my loving husband, Brother Larry Spencer, for weathering the terrible storm with me and allowing God to replace in our marriage what Satan tried to destroy. I love you much.

My son, Brother Nicholas Spencer, I thank God for you every day. I praise the name of the Lord that you are living a life that is pleasing in the eyes of God. I pray that as you continue your walk with Jesus, you grow closer and closer to Him. I love you, Nicholas.

Mother Dear, a mother's love is unconditional and I can say that the love you have for me is just that. You have never judged me for the decisions I made while I was living in the world and now that we both are saved we support each other in our walk with God. You're my mom, my best friend, and my prayer partner. I love you, Mother.

Sugarbabe, as the first-born child, you were always the leader in charge of Pookey and me. Daddy and Mother Dear expected you to do a fine job of watching over us and I must say you always did. Now that we are grown, you are still leading by example. The day you decided to be baptized in the name of Jesus and receive the gift of the Holy Ghost I saw a big change in you. I saw how peaceful you were and how much you enjoyed attending Bethesda Temple Church. I praise the name of the Lord for you and I truly enjoy our walk with the Lord together. I love you, big sister.

Pookey, no matter how many times you and your family have had to relocate because of your husband Gary's job, we have always talked on the phone and visited each other. However, our talks became different once I became saved. Pookey, I live for the times that I talk with you on the phone witnessing to you on the goodness of the Lord. I praise the Name of the Lord for He words my mouth with what I need to say to you in order for you to receive His message. As each day passes, I can see your desire for God in your life grows stronger and stronger. Pookey, it won't be long before you and your family are baptized in the name of Jesus and filled with the gift of the Holy Ghost. When that day comes, my spirit will rejoice. Pookey, little sister, I love you.

Barb, I remember the first day we met and we both said for some reason it was meant for us to be friends. Well, after all we have been through, we both know that it was God who brought us together. I thank God for you, Barb, because you have always been there for me. Some people define the word friend as a person that they talk to on occasion, or if they happen to work at the same place, they only talk to each other at work. In other words, at 5:00 P.M., friendship ends and it doesn't begin again until 8:00 A.M. Barb, you're not my friend, you're my sister. Thank you for praying for me and with me when Satan was busy setting traps for me. I love you, Barb and I am so blessed to have you in my life.

I would like to thank my faithful prayer warriors Sister Rosie E. Douglas, Sister Earline A. Helm, Sister Artimese L. Johnson, and Sister Ida M. Flanigan who prayed for me without ceasing.

I would like to thank my praise saints who gave me words of encouragement as I wrote the Lord's book. They are; Minister Julian and Melanie Johnson, Sister Angela Anderson, Sister Shirley Houston, Sister Francis Douglas, Sister Cindy Casey, and Sister Marva Houston.

1

In the Beginning

In the beginning, God put together Earl Douglas and Rosie Bailey to form Mr. & Mrs. Earl and Rosie Douglas. They were married April 8, 1956. Earl and Rosie had three children. Their names were Earline Anita Douglas, Karen Denise Douglas, and Juanda Jean Douglas. This story is about me, Karen Douglas.

I was born in 1960 in St. Louis, Missouri. Life in the Douglas household was just little short of living on an army base. My father was a very strict man. He was a no-nonsense type of character. It was either his way or no way at all. Daddy was a manager for the U.S. Post Office. That was something to be very proud of because for a black man to get a job with the postal service and work his way to the top was quite an accomplishment.

Daddy was used to making all decisions on his job. When he returned home, he didn't know how to remove the hat of authority and replace it with the hat of a family man. Daddy had a major problem. He was an alcoholic. To look at him you would have never guessed. He didn't fit the typical description of an alcoholic. As I look back, I now understand that my father suffered from low self-esteem. He truly enjoyed making someone feel as if they were beneath him. Anytime he had a chance to put you on Front Street he did.

My mother is one of the kindest people you would

want to know. Her career was in nursing. She worked at St. Mary's Hospital for many years before finally retiring. I always wondered what my mom saw in my dad. Talk about opposites attracting. Mother didn't drink, use foul language, and was family oriented. She was everything Daddy wasn't. I don't know how she was able to balance the stress of work with the stress of living with him. Don't get me wrong, I loved my father, I just didn't like his ways. My mom was always the peacemaker in the house. No matter how bad things would get around the house, mother always had a way a making everything seem alright. I have to wonder sometimes if she knew what true happiness really was.

I recall many days and nights my father would pick fights with my mother for some of the craziest things. If I close my eyes, I can still hear all the loud fussing, cussing, things being thrown around, and my mother crying. When my dad wasn't fighting with my mom, he was busy at work talking about his daughters. All three of us girls were treated terribly but for some reason I was treated the worst. Earline was always very smart in school. She was always on the honor roll and learning came very easy for her. Juanda was a clone of Earline. Juanda was always on honor roll and learning came easy to her, too. Then there was me. I had a learning problem.

In those days teachers, let alone parents, knew nothing about learning disabilities. All they knew was to call your child slow. In my father's vocabulary, the word slow translated to dumb, stupid, lazy, and not trying hard enough. I can recall many a day he would get me in front of my sisters and my mother and rake me over the coals about how I would never amount to anything. He would say the only thing I would ever be good at was cleaning dirty toilets because that didn't require any thinking. Talk about damaging my self-esteem. I had none at all. Period.

Holidays and weekends were always the worst around the Douglas household. This was free time for Daddy to drink, drink, and drink some more. Let the alcohol and the temper mix and ferment together and before you know it, you've got a time bomb waiting to explode. We all learned fast just stay out of his way and when he came home to run and hide. For the rest of my youth, young teens and late teens my life was not happy. I realize my father didn't like himself but he couldn't admit to that. So, he took the coward's way out and made everyone else, especially me, always second guess myself, have severely low self-esteem and not feel I was worthy of anything good.

I have since learned to forgive him for all he had done. What's really sad is that I have to wonder if my father was ever really happy or if he even knew what the word meant. As with every beginning there has to be an end. The end for my father came on April 26, 1997. He lost his battle with cancer. I wish I could say that Daddy was a changed person before he died but that would only be a lie. He was still talking down to my mother and giving her a hard time. I'm sure in his own way he loved her as only he knew how but you have to feel sorry for a person who waits until his last few months to tell his loved ones how sorry he is. I had to wait until my father was almost dead before I heard him say I love you. At least he said it. Easy words yet for some reason, for some people, they're the hardest words to say.

2

The Lord Said, "The Fourth Hymn You Will Die"

In 1967, I experienced something that an ordinary person, let alone a child has probably never encountered. I was seven years old and sound asleep in my bed. I shared the same room with my sister Juanda. She was asleep and never saw or heard a thing. A bright light appeared before my eyes. It was the brightest light I had ever seen. I was awakened by the light and the sound of a voice. The voice, I knew it was the Lord, said, "The fourth hymn you will die." In the blink of an eye, the light and the Lord's voice were gone. I remember jumping out my bed and running as fast as I could to my parents' room. I was crying and told my mother what the Lord told me. My mom told me not to worry. She said nothing was going to happen to me. What else could a mother tell her child? All she knew was she had to settle down her hysterical daughter—and what better way than saying everything was going to be alright?

I went back to my room and told both my sisters what had happened. All three of us were worried because as usual we would be attending church service and the thought of me dying after the fourth hymn stayed on all of our minds. We all were dressed and left for church, all three following behind our mother. Once at church, we were singing hymns. The fourth hymn came and as the church was singing, us three girls looked at each other with a look of panic upon our faces. As I recall, my mom had a look of worry on her face, too. After all, she had promised me nothing was going to happen. I held my breath as the last word was sung, waiting and anticipating the worst. Nothing happened. My mother was right. All that worry for nothing. I forgot about the visit from the Lord that day, however, I never really forgot it for good.

3

She May Have Had a Stroke

The year was 1983. The month was October. Things were going great for me. I was twenty-three years old and employed by the University City Police Department as a police and fire dispatcher. It was Friday and I was getting off from work and was en route to my apartment to take my mother out for her birthday dinner. I was feeling great and excited about my evening and a chance to spend some quality time with Mom. I picked her up and we headed out to Stuart Anderson's Cattleman and Co. This restaurant was one of the best places to eat if you wanted a great steak.

We ordered our food and sat back and talked about the day's happenings. I remember telling Mother how happy I was that we were together sharing her birthday. It meant a lot to me that I could afford all by myself to treat her to dinner. We ate our meal and had dessert. I returned her home around 10:00 P.M. I remember Daddy asking if we had a good dinner. I told him everything was great and Mother said she really enjoyed herself. I kissed them both goodnight and drove off to my apartment.

Saturday morning I awoke and I was very excited. I met one of the U. City police officers and that night we were going out for dinner. I had errands to run and grocery shopping to do. I also wanted to allow some time to shop for a new outfit.

6

Six o'clock rolled around and Larry Spencer was knocking at my door. He looked great and he told me how beautiful I looked. We dined at Red Lobster. The evening was full of great conversation and great company. We were both on the afternoon shift and decided to make it an early evening. He walked me to my door and kissed me good-night. He said, "I'll see you at work."

Sunday morning. My clock rang at 10:00 A.M. I tried to get out of bed, however, I had problems moving my legs. They felt heavy, as though they weighed a ton. I managed to get out of bed and get myself dressed. Don't ask me why, but for some reason I wanted to see if I could feel anything in my legs. I grabbed a safety pin and stuck myself. I could barely feel the pin stick. I called Larry and told him what had happened. He came over and noticed I was having a hard time walking. I told him that I could not feel the pointed stick of a pin I was holding. He tried sticking me and I had no feeling. Larry drove me to work with him. He went upstairs for roll call and I went into the dispatcher's office to begin work.

I remember trying to pick up a pencil to write down what time I wanted to eat lunch. I couldn't pick up the pencil. Toni Adams, one of the dispatchers, called over to the fire house and asked the paramedics to come over and take a look at me. Upon their arrival, I was getting weaker and weaker. I was having problems moving my arms and hands. The paramedics checked me out and said that I might have had a stroke. They were going to transport me to Barnes Hospital. I asked Toni to please let Larry know what was going on.

The time was 4:00 P.M. I was at Barnes Hospital, scared to death. My primary physician, Dr. Gerald O' Connell, was called and told what had happened to me. Dr. Sven Ellison, the chief of neurology, greeted me. Dr. Ellison took me into an examining room and discovered I was having problems moving my arms and legs. He ordered a series of tests: blood tests, motor skills, CT scan, and spinal tap. I remember one of the nurses dialed my parents' home and while she was holding the phone I took a deep breath and in the bravest voice possible, I told my mom that I was at Barnes Hospital and all I knew was that I was having problems moving my arms and legs.

My parents arrived at the hospital and were shocked to see me. How could their daughter who kissed them goodnight less than forty-eight hours ago now be lying in a bed not able to move? The time was 6:00 P.M. I was completely paralyzed from the neck down. Dr. Ellison came into my room and set a tray of food in front of me. He told me to pick up the fork and start eating. I looked at the fork. My mind told me to pick it up however, I could not. For some reason I couldn't move my arms, hands, or legs.

Monday morning Dr. O'Connell came in bright and early to see me. I asked him what was wrong with me. He told me the results of my test should be in today and he along with Dr. Ellison would tell me what was going on.

Larry came in to see me. I could tell by the look on his face he was upset. He was trying so hard not to let me see how worried he was. I had informed him that the doctors had not yet received word on what the results of my test were. My parents and Larry were in the room with me. The room was crowded but not a word was being spoken. Both my doctors came into my room with the results of my test. They told me that the test had ruled out Guillain-Barre, amyotrophic lateral sclerosis otherwise known as Lou Gehrig's disease, and at that time multiple sclerosis. They told me I had transverse myelitis. I had no idea what that disease was; I only knew that what it was doing to my body was serious.

I remember Larry telling me what Dr. Ellison asked him. Dr. Ellison asked Larry if he was serious about me and our relationship because if he wasn't now would be a good time to leave me. You might think the nerve of this doctor to ask Larry this question but in hindsight Dr. Ellison was really looking out for my best interests. I could only imagine what kind of pressure this must have put on Larry. We hadn't been dating long and Dr. Ellison asked him a question like this. Even if he wanted to leave how could he? All eyes were on Larry. Thank God he stayed right by my side.

4

Road to Recovery

Being told I had transverse myelitis was the easy part. Learning how to walk again was one of the hardest challenges I had to face. Barnes Hospital had an excellent rehab center. There, physical therapists did what they were trained to do. That was to get you to walk again. I can understand how a baby feels learning how to walk. It's a scary feeling. I felt like I was going to fall even though the therapist had a belt around my waist. I was determined I was going to be successful and I would be walking again real soon. I had all my family and friends praying for me.

I remember how my family would come to the hospital every day and cheer me on during my rehab sessions. Even when I had a bad day, they were my biggest fans. I don't know if they knew this but hearing them cheer me on was one of the reasons I was determined to keep trying. The love they showed me was enough to motivate me into doing anything. At that point, nothing seemed impossible. The other reason I was determined to walk was Larry. He was my next biggest fan. You see, I expected my family to be there for me no matter what. But Larry was different. We had just started dating and I was unsure if he would stay or leave. At that point I didn't really want to know. All I know is that I enjoyed his company and was happy to see him each and every day.

Dr. Ellison told me I was ready to be released. I would be able to finish my physical therapy on an outpatient basis. My release from the hospital was just the beginning of what lay ahead of me. In 1983, there was no Americans with Disabilities Act. In other words, getting around in a wheelchair was almost impossible. There were no bathrooms that were handicapped accessible. If you had to enter a building that had steps, you would have to pull the person up the stairs while in the wheelchair. You get the picture?

Having to use a wheelchair to get around was like a punishment. However, that never stopped my family from taking me out. There were many times my mom would get me dressed and my dad would put me in the wheelchair and wheel me out to the car. He would have to lift me up and place me in the seat. He would then have to disassemble the wheelchair and pack it in the trunk. It would have been much easier just to have me sit at home but my family wouldn't hear of that. I thank God for them.

Larry and I were still dating. He came over to my parents' house every day to visit me. We would go to the movies, out to dinner, or just take a stroll. He was never embarrassed to be seen with me in public. I must give you a visual picture of what I looked like. If you know anything about the medication Prednisone, you know that it makes you gain weight and retain fluid. Well, I was on a very high dose of this medication. My weight before I became ill was 160 lbs and I wore a size 10. At six feet, I thought that was a nice size. Now that I was on Prednisone, I went from weighing 160 lbs to weighing 220 lbs and wearing a size 24. My hair had fallen out, too. In my opinion, I looked a mess. But in the eyes of Larry, I was still beautiful.

Larry told me he loved me very much and I loved him. Neither of us knew what the future would hold for us. We didn't know if I would ever get out of the wheelchair but for some reason that was the least of our worries. Larry asked me to marry him. My first thought was that I must have imagined him asking me. I asked him to repeat what he just said.

He said, "Will you marry me?"

Of course I said yes. I thought to myself, *How lucky am I? I'm paralyzed, in a wheelchair, I weigh 220 lbs, lost most of my hair, and Larry wants to marry me.* My parents were just as excited as I was. They really liked Larry a lot. After all, he stayed right by my side and they could tell that he really did love me.

5

In Sickness and in Health

The year was 1985, it had been two years since I was diagnosed with transverse myelitis. Larry had asked me to marry him and life for the most part was great. My mother and I were busy picking out bridesmaids' dresses and of course my dress. Even though I was still in my wheelchair, most of the time, getting around didn't seem as difficult as before. That's probably because I was so excited to be getting married.

Larry and I decided to have a small wedding party. I had both my sisters in the wedding. The oldest, Earline, was the matron of honor and Juanda, the youngest, was a bridesmaid. Larry chose his dad, Loren, to be the best man and Lonnie Krammer was a groomsman. We thought it would be best to keep it simple because I was still in my wheelchair and I didn't want a wedding with all the bells and whistles and me having to be rolled down in a wheelchair by my father. Daddy was busy taking care of the financial part of the wedding. He asked me all the time if I was happy and of course I told him YES. I knew he was just as happy as I was.

The day of the wedding finally arrived. All my family from out of town were there and I was so excited. I had been praying all along for the Lord to bless me with being able to walk down the aisle with my father instead of having to go down in my wheelchair. I bought shoes with heels and intended to walk in them. Everyone was where they were supposed to be. My sisters looked beautiful and so did my mother. When the music started playing for my father and me to enter, I was nervous. My feet and legs felt like they were in blocks of cement. I can close my eyes and see my arm locked around my dad's arm. He asked me if I was ready. I said yes.

Daddy said, "Hold on to me real tight and we will walk slow. Don't worry about a thing, I've got you." As we walked into St. James Church, the crowd started to stand. I remember thinking to myself, *Look at everybody standing for me.* My dad looked very handsome that day and I could tell he was very proud to be escorting me down the aisle. All the problems I had seemed not to even matter. I was about to become Mrs. Larry Spencer. I never thought I would see this day. When Pastor Mantaufaul introduced us to the church as Mr. and Mrs. Larry Spencer, I just wanted to freeze time and remember how great I felt. We had a great reception with lots of food, drinks, and music. Everyone seemed to have a great time. Larry and I couldn't afford a honeymoon, however, we went to the Westport Plaza Hotel and that was as great as any honeymoon. I could have cared less where we went as long as I was with Larry.

I had just gotten all the thank-you notes mailed out when I became ill again. I had to go back into the hospital because I became weaker and was experiencing problems with my vision. Dr. Ellison was again my doctor and he and Dr. O'Connell ran more tests. They later discovered that what they thought was transverse myelitis was really multiple sclerosis. Being diagnosed with MS was far worse than transverse myelitis. Imagine this. We've just been married for about seven weeks and now it feels like someone has just dropped a bomb right in my lap. How could this be? This was not supposed to happen. I was told I had transverse myelitis and with time I would walk again. Now that I had MS who knew what each day would bring? Thank God for my husband Larry. He was right by my side but I could see the hidden signs of worry. Worry about how we would make ends meet. Worry about how he could take care of me and work as a police officer. The last thing he needed was more stress to go along with the stress he already had from his job.

I was not able to work at all. This put a huge financial burden on Larry. We had just purchased a new Chrysler convertible. It was our dream car, however, our dream car was going to have to go back. We couldn't afford it. Larry called the dealer and told them what had happened to me. They told us to pay what we could when we could as long as we made a monthly payment. We were able to keep the car. What a blessing this was. That was just one of our many financial problems.

Lucky for us, Larry and I lived in Canterbury Garden apartments and back then, if you were a University City police officer and patrolled the property, you could live there for half the price of the rent. That's what we did. Larry has always been good at managing money. He really had no choice but to be good. He was the only person working and he had to make sure we had enough money to pay all of our bills. I hated being sick. I was in and out of my wheelchair so much that I could not get a job. Can you imagine the amount of stress this put on our marriage? We were newlyweds. This was not supposed to happen.

In 1986, we had saved enough money to buy our own house. That was the great news. The bad news was I had gotten sicker. My parents would take turns with Larry coming over to our house and taking care of me while Larry was at work. I could sense that the stress from taking care of me was starting to get to Larry. He had to feed me, bathe me, dress me, put me on the bed pan and anything else I needed to survive. All this responsibility was thrown upon Larry and he still had to face his job at work. I thank God for giving me such a wonderful husband. In the twenty-one years that I had been sick, Larry only had one blow up. It's funny now but it was not funny then. He was fixing me dinner. For the past four days I had eaten tuna fish. I asked Larry could I have something else to eat instead of tuna because I was tired of eating that. He got so mad that he started shouting and screaming. He threw the tuna out and told me to get my dinner my own self. He knew I could not have done that because I was too weak. He stormed out of the house and left me there lying in the bed hungry.

While he was at work, he told me he felt so bad. I knew he didn't mean to do what he did. It was the stress of having a wife depend totally on you to help her, all the finances dumped into your lap, and wondering if you made a mistake in marrying. My mom and dad came over. Mother fixed me something to eat while Daddy and I talked. Daddy said he understood how Larry felt even though he didn't like what had happened.

Larry came home from work and you could feel the tension in the house. My parents left, although they were reluctant to do so. Larry began to cry as he told me how sorry he was. He explained how stressed out he was over my MS and all the responsibilities that went along with just taking care of me. He said he loved me and he was sorry. I was crying too and I knew how he must have felt. It's a lot of work taking care of someone sick, while working and taking care of all the bills. We were just married and it seemed like after we said "I do" that's when all hell broke loose. This was just the beginning of our problems. We have always had to struggle with having enough money to pay bills and still afford to buy groceries. It seemed like all the happiness I felt in the beginning of my marriage was slowly being buried by problems, problems, and more problems.

6

In Good Times and Bad Times

It was now 1989. I was out of my wheelchair and I was even working. I was beginning to feel somewhat independent now that I had my own money. This could be a good thing and also a bad thing. Earlier, Larry and I had such great problems with our finances that we were not able to do anything. Now I know that my illness was the contributing factor to our problems but now that I had a job I didn't want to hear Larry say we couldn't afford this or that. Now that I felt stronger here came the devil sticking his ugly head into our affairs. For those of you who don't know this, the devil has a job. He's good at what he does. He comes to kill, steal, and destroy. All of which he's very capable of doing. As I stated earlier, now that I was feeling better and had a job, I felt like I was ready to go out and have some fun.

Larry and I had problems in our marriage as all people do. One of our problems that always seemed to cause tension was his two boys from his previous marriage. Danny and Jeff were great kids. As I look back now, I realize that I was a selfish, insecure, person who didn't want Larry spending any time with his own kids. You see, I thought that if he spent time with the kids it meant that he still loved their mother, his ex-wife. I thought Larry would love them more than me. And for me, that was a problem. I remember one particular time I had to go back into the hospital. It was during Larry's vacation and he had the boys for the next week. I can remember asking Larry to come and visit me in the hospital. I had been there two days and he hadn't come to see me. He stated that he was with his boys and told me that he didn't think that he would be able to come and visit. That statement not only killed me, it killed our relationship. I held that statement against Larry and it was that statement that put a wedge in our marriage. I guess we were both looking for a reason to put some distance between us.

When I left the hospital, I was a different person. I decided that since my husband didn't come visit me in the hospital then I would no longer have a husband. What did that really mean? In my world that meant that I was free to do what ever I wanted to because I wasn't married. This goes back to what I said earlier. The devil stuck his head into our lives and I was out to hurt Larry for not coming to see me. As I look back on things, it would have been much easier to just share with Larry how he hurt me and we could have worked things out. But that wasn't in the plan. Larry says to this day he had no idea that I was getting him back for hurting me. I have to admit I was good at what I did in not letting him think I was angry at him. I had to justify what I was about to do and in my world I was right and he was wrong.

Now you know the devil always likes to tempt us with what we don't have. What I didn't have was money. So what happened was that I met a man: not just any man, but a man with money. Not only did he have money but he had a fancy car, a new big house, fine clothes and lots of charm. It was all very impressive for a woman twenty-nine years old or for that matter any woman who was looking for a man to take the hurt away. His name was Kurt Englander.

He was a man who had lots of charm, class, and money. I met him at a club and we danced the night away. I took his number and told him I would call him later. In the beginning I told Kurt that I wasn't married. Although later I told him the truth. I looked at Kurt as the man who would make me forget about Larry. After all, in my world Larry was the reason I was looking for someone else. If he hadn't hurt my feelings this would have never happened. You see how the devil can make you rationalize any situation in your favor to keep you doing wrong?

I began an affair with Kurt. He took me out different places. Places I had never been. His class of people was far different from what I had been used to. He socialized with judges, politicians, lawyers, and doctors. I just knew in my head that I had hit the jackpot. All my problems were about to disappear. Larry and I were growing further and further apart. Neither of us tried anymore. It was as if we were living two separate lives. We lived in the same house under the same roof but that was it. Nothing else.

As Kurt and I continued dating, I noticed certain things that I shall call red flags. I know you have heard the saying, "All that glitters isn't gold," or "The grass always looks greener over the other side of the fence," haven't you? Well I'm here to tell you no, the grass on the other side of the fence is in far worse condition than yours. All the charm that Kurt displayed soon turned into control and possessiveness. All of a sudden our relationship wasn't fun anymore. We began fighting. I told him I had never been a woman that would allow a man to tell me what to do. I thought that we could work it out because like I said Kurt had the type of money I liked, the right type of social class of people I wanted so much to be a part of, the good life, with the fancy car and the nice clothes. It was all about image for me at that point.

Then the day came. In May of 1989, I found out I was pregnant with Kurt's baby. What was I going to do? I knew Kurt had some very serious issues and I also knew that

Larry and I weren't being intimate. So what did I do? I did what any woman in my situation would do. I started having sex with my husband. I remember telling Larry that I felt sick and nauseous. I told him let's get a pregnancy test to see if I'm pregnant. We did and of course the results were positive. Now he thought I was pregnant with his child. Now I know you're wondering what I told Kurt. Kurt wanted me to have an abortion. He was a forty-four-year-old man who had never been married and he didn't expect this to happen. He hadn't planned on being a dad and for him, me having an abortion would just make his life easier. So I told him I was going to have an abortion and I never wanted to see him again. Being pregnant brought Larry and I right back together again. I had since forgiven him for not coming to see me in the hospital and as far as he knew, we were expecting a new baby. I thought I had gotten away with my affair and Kurt was out of my life forever.

For most of my pregnancy, I kept a very low profile, hoping not to run into Kurt. One day I decided to go with a girlfriend of mine to listen to some jazz. As luck would have it I ran into Kurt. He saw that I was very much pregnant and knew that I did not have the abortion I told him I was going to have. He told me that he had changed and he wanted us to be a family. I told Kurt under no circumstances would I leave Larry for him. I told him he had already shown me his true colors and in the words of my father years ago, "A leopard never loses his spots." What that means is that people are who they are. If they display behavior that you don't like don't think for one minute they can change without the Lord in their lives. And believe me, I knew Kurt wasn't about to change. He told me if I didn't let him know when the baby was born, he would tell Larry everything.

The day arrived. It was show time. On Sunday February 11, 1990, Nicholas Patrick Spencer was born at 10:03 P.M.

20

Larry was right at my side and all was well. When I came home from the hospital, I called Kurt as I had promised. He saw Nicholas several times, however, I didn't think Kurt wanted the responsibility and all that came along with being a father. For the next three years, Larry, Nicholas, and I were able to enjoy ourselves as a family with Kurt only having very limited visits with Nicholas.

7

The Angel

Nicholas was now three years of age. Kurt hadn't made any problems and Larry thought Nicholas was his child. After all, why would he think differently? Two major events occurred in 1993 that changed my life completely. One event opened my eyes and one made me want to run and hide. I'll share with you the good one first.

Larry, Nicholas, and I were all at Stacey Park. I was on my cane because I was having some problems with my MS. Larry and Nicholas were playing tag and running around. I was seated on the park bench enjoying myself, watching my family having fun when all of a sudden, out of nowhere a lady came running up to me. She had on a jogging suit and said she was all out of breath. I told her that running will do that to you.

She said, "I've been looking all over for you."

I said, "For me?"

She said, "Yes."

She began to tell me, "The Lord hears the prayers of yours and others. He knows how much pain you're in. He will heal you completely but now is not the time. The Lord has some work for you to do."

I turned my head to motion for my husband to look and when I turned back to where the lady had been standing, she was gone. I knew that was an angel from the Lord delivering me His message. I got home and told my whole family what had happened. At that time the only people in my family who were saved, by that I mean who were baptized in the name of Jesus and filled with the Holy Ghost, were my mother's two sisters Aunt Tee and Aunt Dinka as well as my Big Mama. They all told me that the woman who spoke to me was, in fact, an angel. They told me to always hold on to what the angel said, no matter what happened. Now to a person who isn't saved yet those words really don't mean that much. However, I must say that periodically the words that the angel spoke to me did cross my mind. I never forgot what she said.

That same year Larry was handed some news by way of messenger delivery that I thought would never surface. Larry found out that Nicholas was not his son. Kurt had thrown me a curve ball. He never told me he was taking us to court to establish paternity and file for joint custody of Nicholas. I still have Larry's facial expression etched in my mind when I came home from the store and Larry threw the court papers at me. My heart skipped a beat.

How could this have happened? How could I have not seen this coming? What was I going to tell Larry? My first thought was to lie. *That's it, I'll just tell another lie.* Then I decided to tell the truth. I told him about the affair and all about Kurt. I told him why it happened. Being the great man Larry is, he didn't want to dwell in the past. We had only a month before we were to appear in court to defend ourselves against Kurt. We needed to find an attorney but first we needed $2,000. The only people who had that type of money were my parents. That meant I had to tell my parents the truth about Nicholas' paternity. For some reason, it was harder to tell my parents, especially my father, than it was to tell Larry. We went to my parents' house under the pretense that I would tell them what happened. I got a far as saying,

"Daddy" and I froze. Larry had to continue and he told the whole story.

I think my father was in some kind of denial because after Larry finished, my dad asked us, "What does this have to do with Nicholas?"

Larry said, "Dad, what I'm trying to tell you is that I am not Nicholas' father. Kurt is. We need the money from you in order to fight him in court."

My father gave me a look that made me feel cheap and dirty. He never said a word again about what I did and they gave us the money.

We went to court represented by our attorney Armenta D. Cotton. She was a dynamite attorney and wasn't intimidated by Kurt or his attorney. Paternity was established and the trial was less than two weeks away. I was praying to the Lord that He would not allow Kurt to have joint custody nor would he allow the judge to change Nicholas' last name from Spencer to Englander. I didn't want everybody in my family to find out the truth. Praise the Lord. He answered my prayers. The judge denied joint custody and also denied permission for name change. I thanked the Lord for answering my prayers. I think that is when it hit me like a ton of bricks. I realized I needed to pray to God whenever my son was involved with anything having to do with Kurt. My door to God was starting to open. I praise His holy name. Thank you, Jesus.

Now perhaps you're wondering what happened to Kurt? Well, he didn't succeed in what he set out to do. First, Kurt wanted to break up my marriage to Larry by having the court papers delivered to him. However, his plan backfired. What he tried to destroy only made Larry and I stronger. Second, he wanted joint custody and the name change. He didn't get anything. As years went on, Kurt had us in and out of court for everything from modifying child support to me calling him names in public and in front of Nicholas, to me not allowing him to see Nicholas, not changing Nicholas' middle name officially on his records to Englander, and so on.

For a man who claims to have such a busy life it certainly doesn't seem like it. All the times Kurt worried about what I wasn't doing, he must have forgotten to pay his child support. He wanted all the rights entitled to him but he didn't want to pay his support. In the next chapter you will read about the most important court case involving Kurt and I.

8

Fourth of July

This chapter is probably the most powerful chapter in the whole book next to me receiving the Holy Ghost, for it was the reason I decided to trust God to make a way out of no way.

It was the Fourth of July holiday, and Kurt's holiday to have Nicholas. I dropped Nicholas off at Kurt's mother's house on Friday, July 4th to spend the weekend with Kurt. Just to let you know, Kurt and I had a very nasty relationship. We could not be in the same room for very long before we would end up in an argument. So to keep the arguments down, I would drop off Nicholas at Kurt's mother's house and also pick him up from there. This seemed to work out best for all of us, mostly Nicholas. I told Kurt's mother that I would pick him up at 6:00 P.M. on Sunday, July 6th. I kissed Nicholas good-bye and told him I would see him later. Little did I know what lay ahead for Nicholas and me.

Kurt picked Nicholas up early Saturday morning and took him over to his apartment. Around 10:00 A.M. I got a phone call from Kurt asking if he could take Nicholas to Nashville, Tennessee because a friend of his mother died and he wanted to attend the funeral. I asked to speak to Nicholas before I would give a response. Nicholas was very afraid and he started crying. I asked what was wrong and Nicholas stated that he was afraid to go out of town with

Kurt. He begged me not to let Kurt take him. I told Nicholas to put Kurt back on the phone. I told Kurt that there was no way I would let him take Nicholas. While he and I were arguing on the phone, I could hear Kurt scream at Nicholas to shut up all that crying. Kurt hung the phone up on me and I instantly panicked. I called up his mother and told her what had happened. I begged her to please call Kurt and ask him not to take Nicholas out of town. I thought that his mom was someone I could trust. I told her how nervous I was that Kurt might take Nicholas. She assured me that she would talk to Kurt and she told me to relax everything would be alright. I took her for her word, silly me.

Sunday morning came and as I was getting ready for my part-time job, I tried not to think any negative thoughts. I only allowed myself to believe Kurt's mother talked to him and at 6:00 P.M. I would be picking Nicholas up from his mother's house. I got to work and around 10:00 A.M. my husband called and stated that Nicholas called him at home and told him that he and Kurt would be leaving for Nashville, Tennessee and they would be back sometime Wednesday afternoon. I recall letting out a loud scream, and telling my supervisor what had just happened. I informed him that I had to leave and handle my business. As I got into my car, my first thought was, *Where should I begin looking*? For some reason I thought, I would drive to Kurt's apartment and see if he might be bluffing. All the while I was praying and asking God to watch over Nicholas. I asked God to protect him from any danger and please God don't let Kurt hurt Nicholas in any way.

I arrived at Kurt's apartment and found that they had left. A neighbor stated that he saw them leave with their luggage. My heart sank all the way to the bottom of my toes. I felt like I had just died. All I could focus on was what I could do to get Nicholas back. With nowhere else to turn, I drove myself over to my cousin Carol's house. She is a lieutenant for the University City police department. I had vowed never to let my family know my secret as to the identity of Nicholas' father. But I had a new attitude now. I could care less who knew. Right now all that mattered was that I get Nicholas back.

Carol told me she would do whatever needed to be done to help me. She made a phone call to St. Louis City Police Department 9th District and spoke to the duty sergeant. Carol informed him of what had happened. The duty sergeant informed her to tell me to wait until the time Kurt was supposed to return Nicholas to his mother's house. If Nicholas was not returned by 6:00 P.M. I was to drive down to the police department and file a report. I went home and waited for what seemed like hours. 6:00 P.M. had arrived and Kurt's mother said she had not heard from Kurt. She told me all she knew was that Kurt had taken Nicholas to Nashville. I did as I was told to do. My sister Earline and I went to the 9th District Police Department and waited to file a report. We were greeted by Detective Robert O'Kelley. He was a juvenile detective. I felt at ease when I saw his face. *At last*, I thought, *someone is going to help me get my son back.*

Detective O'Kelley listened to my story. He wrote down information that he needed for my case. He informed me that I needed the court papers that said I had sole custody of Nicholas. He said that once I came back with those papers, they could start working on my case. I left feeling like some progress had been made and I was a little bit closer to getting Nicholas back.

Monday morning was upon me, and I got myself dressed and went to the St. Louis County courthouse to retrieve the court papers I needed. I must say that what seems like an easy task is anything but easy. I had to show my identification and tell the clerk that I wanted my court file to look for some papers. Without knowing where to look, I felt overwhelmed. I stopped and prayed right in the room where there were lots of people and asked God to please show me what papers I needed to bring with me back to the police department. God answered my prayers and I found the correct papers. I photocopied the ones I needed and rushed back to the police department with my sister Earline to show Detective O'Kelley the papers.

Upon our arrival, I was told that Detective O'Kelley was not due to come in until 3:00 P.M. I didn't want to wait until he came in because time was of the essence. Detective Ann Wood came and spoke with Earline and I. I informed her of the situation and handed her the court papers showing I had full custody of Nicholas. Detective Wood told me that Kurt would be charged with parental kidnapping and endangering the welfare of a child.

When Detective Wood heard Kurt's address, she told me she thought that building was used as special housing for mentally unstable people, people being treated for mental problems or drug abuse. She knew this because she was a patrol officer in the 9th District.

Upon learning that Earline was a special education teacher, Detective Wood asked Earline how this situation could impact a child with ADD. Earline told Detective Wood that stress involved could cause increased separation anxiety, it could be harder for a child to focus and concentrate, a child could become more nervous, and it could worsen the ADD. Detective Wood told me that a picture of Nicholas would be faxed to the Nashville Police Department. They would get an address from the phone number I had given them and the Nashville police would be directed to arrest Kurt and take Nicholas into protective custody. I would have to fly to Nashville and pick up Nicholas and bring him home.

I asked Detective Wood about how long this would take. She told me that she would know something by 7:00 P.M. She told me Detective O'Kelley would be in at about 4:00 P.M. and he would take care of the arrest. Detective Wood told me that I looked exhausted, she advised me to go home and let the police do their jobs.

That evening, I made several attempts to contact Detective O'Kelley, none of which were successful. In the meantime, I contacted American Airlines and told them what had happened. I told them that all of my story could be verified by the St. Louis City juvenile division. I told them I didn't have a lot of money, and could not afford the cost of two tickets at such a short notice. Praise the Lord, American Airlines told me that Nicholas and I could fly for free because they wanted to help me out in any way they could so I could get my son back. I had booked the flight to leave on Tuesday, July 8. Through my tears I was thanking God and American Airlines. The time was now 10:30 P.M. and I still had not heard anything from Detective O'Kelley. I left a voice message saying I had made my flight arrangements to pick up Nicholas and I needed for him to call me back so I would know how to go about picking up my son in Nashville. Detective O'Kelley never did call me back.

I awoke Tuesday morning with a deep pain in my heart. The Lord had made a way for me to pick up Nicholas. All I needed was Detective O'Kelley to call me. I was tired of waiting and called Detective Wood. I left her a voice message telling her that I never did hear from Detective O'Kelley. I asked her to please call me back at work. I called Detective Wood again around 9:45 A.M. I spoke with her. She told me she would see what was going on with my case and call me back and as you probably guessed she never called me back.

Around 10:45 A.M. I went to the office of Major Charles

Adams. I told him if what had happened and asked him if he would please help me out. Being the fine man that he is, Major Adams placed a phone call to the captain of the juvenile division. Major Adams asked him to please find out any information he could concerning my case and to please call him back. The captain said he would be happy to help and said he would call Major Adams back with any information. The captain didn't call back.

I returned back to my desk only to find out Detective Wood had finally called me. I returned her call and she let me speak to Sergeant Harper. Sergeant Harper informed me that nothing was going to be done because "no crime has been committed." He told me there was no "criminal intent" and he hung up on me. I called back and no one would talk to me.

I left work and decided to take matters into my own hands. I went to Kurt's house and parked my car down the street, far enough not to be seen yet close enough to see them. I waited for hours in the heat. About 4:00 P.M., Kurt's car pulled up in front of his apartment with Nicholas inside. My heart was pounding. I called 911 and asked that police be sent to Kurt's apartment so I could get my son back. The police arrived and I was able to get Nicholas back. Kurt was busy screaming at me and calling me bad names. I didn't care what he did. I felt like as long as I had my son back I could care less what happened. I thanked God for helping me. I knew that I had to act fast to keep this from happening again. On July 12th I applied for a child protection order. A summons was issued with a return date of August 24, 2003. I knew I had won the battle but not the war.

9

The Day I Received the Holy Ghost

This is probably the most important chapter in God's book. On August the 15, 2003, I received the Holy Ghost. If you refer back to the second chapter, when God told me I would die after the fourth hymn, I did die. Not physically but spiritually.

I can remember it was a Friday night. It was raining hard outside and around 6:30 P.M. my Aunt Dinka called and said she had Pat Littles on the phone. Pat told me the Lord told her that she had to come over to my house and tonight was the night that I needed to be saved. I recall getting angry and I didn't want to listen to the conversation anymore. I paused and became very quiet. Pat told me again what the Lord told her and let me tell you Evangelist Pat Littles does not play when it comes to preaching the Word of God. She is very serious about salvation and she doesn't back down.

Pat told me the Lord was very clear in telling her today was my day and she and my Aunt Dinka were on their way over to my house. I hung up the phone and told my husband about my conversation. I was angry and didn't want to be bothered. I already knew that I was saved because I went to church every Sunday and my religion, which at the time was Lutheran, didn't believe in the Holy Ghost as a necessity for salvation.

Pat and Dinka arrived at my house around 8:00 P.M. Pat told me that she had just gotten herself some Chinese food and picked out a good sci-fi movie to watch, when the Lord told her to come and work with me. We first sat and just talked about general things. She asked me how my husband was doing. He had just had hernia surgery about a week ago. After several minutes of small talk, Pat sat up in my chair with a very stern look on her face. All of a sudden the laughter stopped. The room was dead silent.

Pat told me the Lord told her that I was dealing with a heavy problem. She told me the Lord told her my son Nicholas was not my husband's child. She told me the heavy burden I had was concerning Nicholas. I broke down in tears and told her she was correct. I shared with her the identity of Nicholas' father and I told her the heavy burden was the court battle I was going to have to face August 24th. I told her how Kurt took Nicholas, without my consent, to Nashville, Tennessee and the court case was to say if Kurt's visitation rights would be suspended or if he would have supervised visitation or if nothing would happen to him at all.

The room was dead silent. Pat told me this was more of a reason for me to be saved and once I receive the Holy Ghost I would receive power and be able to fight. Having listened to her, I still wasn't convinced that I needed God's gift.

One hour had passed by, and I began telling Pat that my religion didn't worship the way she and Dinka worshipped. I told her what most people say when they think they already have the Holy Ghost.

I told her, "I'm nice to people and go out of my way to help everyone."

I told her, "I give money to the church on a regular basis and help people who are less fortunate than myself."

I told her that I had been going to St. James Lutheran Church since I was six years old and Pastor Baker never said anything about receiving the Holy Ghost or being baptized in the name of Jesus. As far as I was concerned, I didn't need what she was trying to tell me. Pat had me open her Bible and along with her we turned to the Book of Acts, Chapter Two, verse one. This talks about the day of Pentecost. She had me to read it first out loud and then to myself. Pat, with great patience, explained to me why this book was important. We then went to thirty-eighth verse, Chapter Two, of Acts and Pat told me I had to be baptized in the name of Jesus. I told her I was baptized in the name of the Father and of the Son and of the Holy Ghost. Pat told me to read Acts thirty-eight again.

She said, with a stern look on her face, "Karen, you need to be baptized in the name of Jesus and receive His gift of the Holy Ghost."

I can remember telling Pat that her Bible must be some kind of trick Bible or better yet her Bible was written for people who practice the Pentecostal faith. Being the patient person she is, she had my aunt Dinka go out to her car and get another Bible. I turned to the same chapters and found the wording to be the same.

It was 11:00 P.M. For three hours, we had been discussing my need to receive the Holy Ghost. Pat sat up in her chair and looked at me straight in my face and said, "I rebuke you, Satan, in the name of Jesus."

She told me not to say another word, just to listen. Amazingly enough, I didn't say another word. Pat told me again I needed to receive the Holy Ghost. I told her with all my problems involving Kurt I would be willing to try to receive God's gift. I remember telling Pat that I had been such a very bad person that God may not want to give me anything. Pat assured me God wanted everyone to receive His gift. She told me all I had to do was to tell God I was sorry for all of my sins. Those sins that I could remember and those that I could not remember. When I had completed that, Pat told me to open my mouth and start breathing. I could feel my mouth move and I started making some sounds. Before I knew it, I was speaking in tongues. God had given me his gift of the Holy Ghost. I spoke for what seemed like a long time. I could hear myself speaking in a different language. I'll tell you this, I'm so glad Pat was obedient to what the Lord told her to do and that she didn't give up on me. On Sunday, August 17, I was baptized in the name of Jesus. I'll tell you the truth, I would never ever want to go back to my old ways of living. Since I was born again, my walk with God gets sweeter and sweeter each day.

As for my court hearing with Kurt, God worked it out so that Kurt signed papers on December of 2003 giving up all his rights to Nicholas. I Praise the Name of the Lord for that.

10

Does the Doctor Always Know Best?

After receiving God's precious gift of the Holy Ghost and being baptized in the name of Jesus, life was great. My blinders had been removed and I was embarking on a new life with my Lord and Savior Jesus Christ. Not long after my new birth, I began to feel a lump in my throat. I was aware something was wrong because when I would eat food, I would have problems swallowing. I was not a stranger to swallowing difficulties, in the past I had swallowing problems stemming from my multiple sclerosis. I was always told by Dr. Douglas Lily that my problems swallowing were related to my MS and not to worry about anything. Of course I believed in every word he said, after all, he was my doctor. All I can say is this time not only was swallowing difficult but I also felt a choking sensation. I got to a point where I was having problems eating food. I would attempt to chew my food up and swallowing only to end up choking and gagging. I became afraid to eat solid food and knew I needed to pay a visit to Dr. Lily.

Dr. Lily examined me and stated my thyroid gland was enlarged. He drew some blood and was going to schedule me for radioiodine uptake. Before I had my radioiodine uptake, Dr. Lily got the blood test results back from the lab. In his letter to me, he stated that my lab work looked good. He said there was nothing wrong with my thyroid. As far as he was concerned this case was closed. The results from my radioiodine uptake showed I had some type of mass in my neck. The doctor stated I would need to have a ultrasound done of my neck in order to get a better picture of what was happening. An ultrasound was scheduled and upon completion, I was told all my tests were going to be forwarded to Dr. Lily. I was informed it would take about three days and I would hear something.

Three days seemed like it was never going to come. My swallowing by now was impossible. I could only swallow liquids. My diet consisted of Ensure and other liquid diet supplements. I began feeling weaker and weaker. My blood pressure had dropped lower than usual. For me, my normal blood pressure was always ninety over seventy. However, my pressure had dropped eighty-five over sixty-five. I remember I started calling Dr. Lily's office after the three-day wait to see what the results of my tests were. I would speak to his nurse and she would tell me that he would get back to me. I called two days later, and to the nurse's surprise, Dr. Lily had not called me back.

She informed me that she would place my test results in the seat of his chair so that in order for him to sit down he would have to move my test results and trigger his memory to call me. Dr. Lily never did call me and I grew weaker and weaker. My blood pressure dropped to seventy over sixty. The color of my skin had gotten very pale and my breathing was very difficult. Whatever was causing me to choke was also obstructing my breathing. I knew I had to do something fast otherwise I was going to die.

I began by praying. I knew God didn't allow me to receive His Gift of the Holy Ghost and be baptized in the name of Jesus only to now allow me to die. No, I knew His plan was far greater than that. The enemy Satan was angry and was trying to kill me by any means possible. Satan knew I would be working for the Lord and he had to stop me. I then called my best friend Barb and told her I didn't feel good. She came and picked me up. I can remember her saying how bad I looked. She drove me to St. John's Hospital where I checked into the emergency room. I told the nurse what my problems were. After getting all important information, I was told to have a seat and wait.

Barb and I arrived at the hospital around 9:30 A.M. I phoned my sister Earline and told her where I was. She joined us at the hospital and waited along with us. I kept asking how much longer of a wait I had and the nurses kept telling me not much longer. Finally, around 1:30 P.M. I was seen by the emergency room doctor. I told him that I was having problems eating any solid food. I informed him of the difficulties I was having in swallowing and of a choking sensation I was feeling. My blood pressure had dropped to sixty-five over sixty and I was weaker than before. The emergency room doctor stated he would call Dr. Lily and see what he wanted to do. After speaking with Dr. Lily, the emergency room doctor informed me that Dr. Lily wanted him to release me and have me come to his office first thing Monday morning.

Barb jumped up out of her seat and told the doctor there was no way she was taking me home. She told the doctor that I was unable to eat solid food and had been surviving off of liquid supplements only. Barb said, "If I take her home she's going to die." It was that statement that made the doctor admit me. He ordered a scan of my neck to be done to determine what was blocking my throat. Once he got the results back, he told me there was some type of large mass in my neck. He didn't really go into detail other than he was going to place me on the floor with patients with different types of cancer. The doctors on that floor are trained to look for certain types of problems involving a mass. Most people would have panicked with just receiving news of this type but I'm not most people. I knew my Father would guide me through whatever storm I had to face.

I thank and praise God for interceding on my behalf and placing such fine doctors in place for me while I was in the hospital. I was seen by Dr. Mark Wallace. He is an oncology specialist who deals with head and neck surgery. After one week in the hospital, and several tests, Dr. Wallace informed me that the mass that was in my neck was not cancer but he was not sure what is was. He did tell me he knew whatever it was had to come out. He released me from the hospital and would schedule me for surgery.

11

Blessed Oil

It was now October, 2003, and my sisters and I were planning my mother's seventieth birthday party. Her party was a very blessed event. We all had a great time celebrating that special day and I thank and praise the name of the Lord for allowing her to see seventy. Everyone was dining on their food and I had a meal of mashed potatoes and ice cream. My appointment to see Dr. Wallace was scheduled for October 5th. My mother went with me to hear what he had to say. As I had stated earlier, Dr. Wallace had told us he didn't really know what was in my neck. He was very honest with me and stated that he would not be able to tell me that I was going to be able to swallow again after the surgery. He made that statement several times. There were no guarantees and he wanted me to be perfectly clear about that before he did the surgery.

My surgery was scheduled for Tuesday, October 14, at 9:00 A.M. I was to arrive at the hospital by 6:30 A.M. Larry and Barb were going to drive me to the hospital but before leaving I packed my blessed oil in my purse. My mother would arrive later, for she had to take Nicholas to school. Around 7:45 A.M., a nurse came to get me to take me to the operation room. I reached inside my purse and placed some blessed oil in my hands. I rubbed them both together and folded them. I didn't want anyone to touch my hands. This oil I had

40

was meant to touch the hands of Dr. Wallace only. I kissed Larry and Barb good-bye and told them both I loved them. I was wheeled into the prep room and that was where Dr. Wallace came and spoke to me. With both my hands I touched the top of his shoulders and shook his hand and I said, "In the name of Jesus, Lord guide his hands as he operates on me. In Jesus' name I pray, Amen." Dr. Wallace assured me all would be fine. I knew everything would be well for I had anointed Dr. Wallace with blessed oil.

What happens next is truly a miracle from God. Dr. Wallace told me while his instrument was placed up to my neck, in preparation for cutting, something told him not to cut there. Dr. Wallace said that the feeling he had was so strong that he moved his instrument down and he said the feeling he had told him to cut there. Once Dr. Wallace opened me up he said he panicked. If he had of cut me where he initially wanted to cut, I would have died. You see, the mass that was in my neck had pulled my carotid artery out of place and therefore Dr. Wallace's incision would have caused my artery to be cut and I would have bled to death. Dr. Wallace thought my surgery would be quick, however, the mass that was cut out of me was wrapped around my artery so tight and also pressing into my esophagus it took longer than anticipated. Dr. Wallace told me the mass was the same size as a golf ball. Imagine the tiny space in your neck and imagine the size of a golf ball. It was only by God's grace and mercy that I survived. Satan thought he could kill me by allowing Dr. Wallace to cut into my neck but God interceded and forced Dr. Wallace to cut lower bypassing my carotid artery. I praise the name of the Lord. When a person is baptized in the name of Jesus and filled with the gift of the Holy Ghost, they are covered by the blood of Jesus. Satan cannot penetrate the covering of the blood no matter how hard or from what angle he tries. I truly believe that had I not received the Gift of the Holy Ghost and **Baptized in the name of Jesus, I would not have survived. This is why this is so important to receive salvation now for tomorrow isn't promised to any of us.**

12

Post-Op

I can remember the first few days after my surgery. I thought about how blessed I was that Jesus guided Dr. Wallace's hands so that he would not cut me where he marked my neck. I'm sure that gave Dr. Wallace something to think about too. Neither he nor I ever discussed the miracle that took place in the operating room; however, we both know and thank Jesus for bringing me through. I would imagine this operation is something Dr. Wallace will never forget.

My birthday was just four days after my surgery. My best friend Barb, along with Nicholas went shopping for my present. My mom and my sister Earline went shopping and bought me a beautiful nightgown since most of my time was going to be spent recuperating. I was exhausted visiting my family and friends. Barb bought me a beautiful bracelet made of crystal stones and a birthday cake. I couldn't eat the cake but I devoured the icing. Larry did a great job taking care of me. He made sure I took my liquid pain medicine on time and attended to my every need. I thank and praise the Lord for my husband, my family, and my friends. I have learned never to take for granted your husband, family or friends because there are so many people less fortunate than I.

I hadn't gone to church yet, however, I thought surely

twelve days was plenty of time to heal enough to go to church. Everybody tried to tell me it was too soon but I wouldn't listen. Larry helped me get dressed and Larry, Nicholas, and I went to church. Well let me tell you this, I wasn't there for more than forty-five minutes when tears began running down my face. I was in pain. Without anyone telling me I told you so, Larry gathered my belongings and we all went home.

I found out from talking to my sister that our church would be having its yearly program. This was like no other program. It was the Holy Ghost Explosion. This event lasted from Thursday, October 30 to Sunday November 2. Great speakers from different churches preached highly anointed sermons. The presence of the Lord would be there in the church and the Holy Ghost moved around freely. This would be my first time attending something like this since I was a new saint. I knew nothing was going to stop me from attending. I went Thursday, Friday, and Sunday. I was able to get my praise on and worship the Lord. Each evening, after the program, I felt better and better. I was so thankful that I went and didn't allow Satan to change my mind. I want to talk about Sunday's program. The name of the visiting bishop escapes me but what he said to me stays etched in my head. Sister Shirley Thomas came over to where I was sitting. She said she wanted me to meet our guest speaker. I wasn't sure why, but I walked with her anyway to meet him. It was a long line of saints waiting to talk with Bishop. Shirley pushed her way up to the front of the line and told Bishop she wanted me to meet him.

Bishop looked at me and placed his hand on top of my head. He began to speak in tongues and when he finished he said, "Satan is terrified of you. God will use you to do His work in a mighty way."

Everyone who was standing around us heard what he

said and they all looked at me. I turned and walked away and I remember telling Shirley, "I don't know why Satan would be terrified of me. I've only been saved for two months. I don't think God would want to use me because I'm too new."

Sister Shirley told me to take what the bishop said and hold on to it. She said in time what he told me would all come to pass. I gave her a look like as if to say, *Right. God's going to use me to do His work. I don't think so.*

November 8 is a day that will stay in my mind forever. Remember what I told you Bishop said to me about how God would use me in a mighty way, well, while I was in the shower, God spoke to me. He said, "First your son Nicholas will be saved, then Larry. After they are saved, you will do work for Me."

God told me this would happen very soon. People listen, Nicholas received the gift of the Holy Ghost on Christmas Day. He was baptized in the Name of Jesus on December 28, 2003. Larry received the gift of the Holy Ghost on Wednesday, January 7, 2004. He was baptized in the Name of Jesus that same day at church. My family was now saved and my work for the Lord had begun.

On Sunday, February 22, 2004, the Lord gave me the words to put together my testimony about how He guided Dr. Wallace's hands throughout the entire surgery. I talked about how I anointed my hands with Blessed Oil and touched Dr. Wallace's hands. After my testimony, Bishop Johnson asked if anyone wanted to be saved. Thirteen souls were baptized in the Name of Jesus and ten received the Holy Ghost. I Praise the Name of the Lord. I still have saints come up to me and tell me how blessed they were just from hearing my testimony. I told them I give God all the glory and all the praise for He is worthy. This is only the beginning of my work for the Lord.

13

Just Walk

I had just completed my powerful testimony in February, and lo and behold I was still having problems with my swallowing. I had to pay another visit to Dr. Wallace. He arranged for me to have what was called a cookie swallow and a barium swallow. He was wondering why I was still having problems swallowing after the long and intense surgery he had performed. My test was scheduled for Monday, March 15, 2004 at St. John's Hospital. I remember leaving the hospital and wondering to myself what my results would be.

It wasn't long before Dr. Wallace called me to his office. He stated that there was still some swelling from the surgery and he reminded me that before the operation, he had made it very clear to me that I might never be able to swallow again. I went to see him again, in May, because I had developed what he called thyroiditis. I can remember how painful this was. Dr. Wallace asked me how my swallowing was coming. I told him that I was still unable to chew food and swallow. Dr. Wallace remained optimistic however, he told me outside of a miracle, I would never be able to swallow food again. He stated that he had done all he could do. Now you're probably wondering what was going on in my head when he made this statement. A part of me was thinking, *What if I can never eat food again what will I do, how will I be able to make it? How will this affect the rest of my health?* My mind was moving fast and lots of questions were circling in my brain. But then I pulled myself together and remembered what the angel said to me while I was at Stacey Park. I knew God was going to heal me but I didn't know when. I left the doctor's office thinking to myself, *At least I am alive and I thank God I can eat mashed potatoes, baked potatoes, soft foods, and all the ice cream I want.* I even got to the point where I could blend foods and drink them down. There was no time for pity parties. My life went on and I knew God had equipped me to handle this.

Around the end of May and the first part of June, I began to notice that I had problems walking. My balance had become so bad that I had to resort to wearing knee braces and ankle braces. I made an appointment with my physician, Dr. Jacobson. Dr. Jacobson sent me to Missouri Baptist Hospital where I received a MRI of my knees and ankles. The diagnosis was chondromalacia patellae otherwise known as a degenerative knee cap. I was told I would need physical therapy as part of my treatment. While I was adjusting to the crutches and knee and ankle braces, another problem arose. My sister, Earline, was diagnosed with a bleeding disorder called pseudo-hemophilia. Her physician told her this could be hereditary and she was advised to tell her other sisters to get tested. I phoned Dr. Jacobson and he advised me to make an appointment with a hematologist.

My appointment was set for June 30, 2004, with Dr. Deborah Wienski. No one knew of my appointment with Dr. Wienski except my husband, mother, and sister. On Sunday, June 27, 2004, Larry and I attended a special service at church. While we were waiting for the program to begin, Sister Clark walked up and sat down next to me.

She looked at me and said, "The road to Calvary was very hard for Jesus. He has chosen a path for you to walk.

The doctors will tell you that you have all new diseases and you will have them but don't worry because the Lord will heal you completely, just walk the path."

Larry and I sat and looked at each other in utter amazement. I knew her message was from God because no one from the church knew I was going to the doctor. I praise the Name of the Lord for allowing one of His workers to deliver His message to me.

Wednesday morning came and I must say I was a little anxious as to what Dr. Wienski would find. We met and while she was examining me, she noticed how long my arms were and how double jointed I was. I was able to take my thumb and cross it over behind my knuckle. Several other tests indicated to her that I had ehlers-danlos. Dr. Wienski drew my blood to test for pseudo-hemophilia but she was pretty much convinced that I had ehlers-danlos. She asked me why I was using crutches and braces to walk and my response was that my knees and ankles were so weak, that if I didn't have the aid of these devices walking would be impossible. It took ten days for my results to come back. I was told that I didn't have the blood disorder but I had the ehlers-danlos. Dr. Wienski told me that with this disease, a person develops a bleeding problem. She told me that whenever I required any type of surgery, I was to have the surgeon call Dr. Wienski and she would advise them of my problem. She also told me that ehlers-danlos could also affect my heart so I would need to be checked out by a cardiologist.

As I sat in the chair, trying to absorb all this information, I had a flashback to what Sister Clark told me would happen, it was clearer than ever. Yes, I was told bad news but I stood on God's promise to heal me so no matter what the doctors said, God said He would heal me.

I had to make an appointment with a cardiologist. This

48

doctor was to give me an echocardiogram and tell me the results. I was told a week later that the left valve of my heart was leaking. The doctor told me he would have to watch it closely to make sure things did not get worse. Again, I stood on God's Word that He would heal me so I didn't care what any doctor said.

Sunday morning, July 25, Sister Clark asked me how I was doing and if I had put my crutches down. I told her no, but "I'm standing on the Lord's word and His promise to heal me."

Sister Clark responded by saying, "You've already got the victory just finish His walk."

Brother Solomon spoke to me after service and said the Lord put on his heart to tell me he saw me real soon throwing down my crutches and being healed. I took what Sister Clark and Brother Solomon said and held on tight and continued to believe that God was going to heal me.

Now, as we know, Satan is always waiting to catch us at our weakest point. I was standing on God's promise but I was still reading each and every day the information about the diseases I was just diagnosed with. On Monday, July 26 the Lord spoke to me and said, "Why are you worrying about what the doctors told you? I told you what they were going to say. All you have to do is walk my path and I will heal you completely and bless you beyond your imagination."

The Lord told me not to read any material on my illnesses, and not to discuss my illnesses with anyone. Wanting to obey what God commanded of me, I threw away any and all information pertaining to my illnesses. I told all my family and friends not to ask me anything about how I was feeling or how my illnesses were coming along. I began to focus on God's promise to heal me and I even began telling people at work that God was going to heal me. I could tell from the expressions on their faces that they thought I was either crazy or believing in something that you only read about in the Bible. I didn't care what they said about me or for that matter what they thought about me. All I know is that God said He would heal me and I knew He would.

14

The Miracle

Friday morning, August 6, was just like any other Friday. I drove myself to work and upon arriving, I gathered my crutches and my purse that I hung around my neck, and hobbled myself into work. I continued to tell everyone who would listen to me that God was going to heal me. I often told them that I was going to be healed quicker than they thought. I remember the looks I got from my co-workers. Some of them would look at me as though I was crazy, and yet some of them would look at me with the expression of, *I'm glad you have faith but miracles only happen in the Bible.* My friend Barb was the only one who stood in agreement with me and really believed that God was going to heal me.

Five o'clock came and it was time for me to go home. I said my goodbyes to my co-workers and with my crutches under my arms and my purse around my neck I hobbled out to my car. Saturday came and there was nothing unusual going on. I talked on the phone with my mom and my sisters. I cleaned the house and ran my weekly errands. Saturday night is usually spent picking out what clothes Nicholas, Larry and I will wear to church. I find that it makes Sunday morning go a lot smoother if we all know what we are wearing. After picking out the clothes I took my shower and prepared myself for bed. I read my Bible for a while, prayed and told Larry and Nicholas good night.

I awoke at my usual time on Sunday morning which was 8:00 A.M. I fixed Larry and Nicholas breakfast and I had my usual can of Ensure along with some applesauce. Larry and I were talking about how to celebrate our 19th wedding anniversary. We normally went out for dinner at Tony's restaurant; however since I could not swallow food we had to change our tradition. We decided to go to a movie and come home and exchange gifts.

It was time for us to leave for church. We normally left around 10:15 A.M. Church started at 10:45 but I liked arriving early so I could participate in group prayer and hear the beginning of the praise and worship singers. Bishop Johnson gave the text from the Book of St. Mark, Chapter 16, verses 14–20. It was these verses that he would apply his sermon to. After Bishop Johnson completed his sermon, he did something different. He first asked for all the ministers sitting in the sanctuary to stand up and walk to the front of the church. He then directed the ministers to lay hands upon each saint as they walked up and say to each saint, "In the name of Jesus, you are healed."

Bishop then motioned for all saints to walk up to a minister and let them lay hands on each one. Bishop said, "We should be able to see some sign that Jesus heals today." Bishop said, "Today, someone is going to be healed."

I walked up to receive my healing in the name of Jesus from one of the ministers and when I returned back to my seat I felt different. My aunt Dinka came over to me and she said, "Sister, it won't be much longer before you are healed."

I told Dinka that I knew and we both began to praise the Lord. At the end of church service, around 1:45 P.M., I was walking out to the car. I told Larry and Nicholas that I felt different again. We were going over to my cousins J.J. and Mel's house for a visit. When Larry pulled up in front of their house, I told Larry that I was healed. I took off the four braces that I needed to help me walk and I left my crutches in the car because I knew I didn't need them. I stepped out of the car and I was walking. I began to run and before I knew it, I had run all the way up to the door of J.J. and Mel's house. When I got inside, I began to scream and rejoice. Melanie and J.J. were just as excited as I was. Larry and Nicholas were speechless. Mel's mother was visiting from Atlanta and she learned from her daughter Mel how sick I had been. I ran in circles around and around J.J. and Mel's house. I opened the front door, and walked up and down their street. I even took their son Joseph for a walk.

I came back into the house and called Aunt Dinka. I told her that the Lord had healed me and for her to come over and see how good I was walking. I went back outside and Aunt Dinka said she almost hit a parked car while driving down the street when she saw with her own eyes that I was healed. We all went into the house and I told Mel to give me some food. I knew I could swallow. Mel gave me some chicken and a biscuit and without any hesitation I chewed my food and swallowed it. What God promised me He would do was done. I was healed from the top of my head to the soles of my feet.

Aunt Dinka phoned Bishop Johnson at his home to tell him the good news. Bishop was just as happy as we were. The next persons to tell were my mom, sisters, and my Aunt Tee. They were gone to Texas for my cousin's wedding. I phoned them and told them I had something to show them when they got home. I stood in my cousin's house and gave God all the glory and all the praise. My husband and I hugged each other tight and we both began to cry. We left J.J. and Mel's house to go home.

Mother Dear, Sugarbabe, and Aunt Tee were due to come in around 5:00 P.M. In the meantime I had arranged for

Aunt Dinka, Aunt Shirley, Aunt Scoggie, Aunt Sugar, my cousin Angie and I to meet at my mom's house around 6:30 P.M. Mother Dear phoned me around 6:15 and told me they were home. They were ready to see what I had to show them. Everybody pulled up around the same time. When I got out of the car, my mother, sister, aunts, and cousins, all began to cry. They all saw that God healed me. We went into the house and began to thank God for my healing. It was a very anointed and blessed event. My cousin Marva, from Houston, phoned and wanted to know what the surprise was. When she found out the Lord healed me, she stayed on the phone and joined in our praise and worship to God for healing me. We were all speaking in tongues and the presence of the Lord was right in the midst of us all. If you have never praised the Lord with your extended family I urge you to do so. The remainder of the evening was spent on us giving testimonies out loud of how good God had been to us. The evening ended with prayer and we all departed from my mother's house around 10:30 P.M.

I could hardly wait for Monday morning to arrive. I left work on Friday not able to walk or swallow and now that God had healed me I could do both. At first people didn't notice that my crutches were gone. They had become so used to seeing them under my arms that as far as they knew I was walking with my crutches. I had to stop people and say, "Look at me. I told you all that God was going to heal me but you didn't want to believe it."

I had one man approach me and asked me where my crutches were? I responded by saying I was healed. He asked me who healed me. I looked at him as if he were crazy and told him, "I was healed by Jesus."

As he walked away, he scratched his head and said, "Oh."

Now you would think that people would be excited to

hear that I was healed by Jesus but that was not the case. I hate to say it but some of the same people who thought it was horrible that I couldn't walk or swallow are now the same people who are talking amongst themselves as to whether I was really sick. I praise the name of the Lord for the people who believed that I was healed. It doesn't matter to me if they believed or not. I'm still healed in the name of Jesus.

On Sunday, August 15, I gave my testimony in front of the saints at Bethesda Temple. We all rejoiced in what God had done. We gave Him all the glory and all the praise. Bishop Johnson asked me what I was going to do with my crutches. He wanted to mount the crutches on the wall in our church as a reminder to everyone that God is still performing miracles.

15

Conclusion

I would like to begin by praising the name of my Lord and Savior Jesus Christ for He is worthy of all the praise. He is the center of my life and I am so honored that Jesus chose me to write His Book. I would like to share with you my personal battles with Satan while I was in the process of writing Jesus' Book.

As I stated in chapter fourteen, Jesus healed me on August 8, 2004. On August the 9, the Adversary was busy attacking me with negative remarks from colleagues. Instead of my co-workers being happy that I could now eat, they were filled with disbelief and questioned if I was faking my inability to walk or swallow. I got to a point where I couldn't walk anywhere without having someone ask me questions about my healing in a very sarcastic manner. The same people who claimed they felt sorry for me were now the very same people who were attacking me. I had a person who would come up to my desk almost every day and ask me if I was still able to eat anything I wanted. My response to her was that God doesn't put a Band-aid on anything. He heals. I also told her she didn't have to ask me every day if I was eating.

One week into my healing and I began to notice some problems with my food getting stuck. I began praying to the Lord and asked Him what was going on. The Lord told me before I put anything into my mouth, I was to say this prayer: "Lord, in the name of Jesus, I ask you to purify and sanctify the food I'm about to place inside of my body. In Jesus' name I pray, Amen."

I did exactly what the Lord told me and my swallowing returned to normal. On August 17, Evangelist Pat Littles called me at work. She told me that the Lord told her to call me. The words Pat spoke to me were calming to my spirit. She told me that God had sent her to be my reinforcement. The Lord told Pat that I was being attacked by the people at work. They were waiting for my healing to fail. Pat told me, "No matter what happens, God did heal you."

She told me to stand on my faith and God's Word. After talking to Pat, I felt like a ton of bricks were lifted off of me. I thanked the Lord for allowing Pat to deliver His message to me and I felt strong again and ready for spiritual battle.

I would like to mention a particular person who talked about me faking my illness and she said that God didn't heal me because I was never that sick. I found out she made that statement on August 19. I passed that same woman on August 20, and her mouth was twisted. You see, since she used her mouth as a weapon against God, He twisted her mouth as a chastisement. It wasn't until the second week in September when she approached me and said quietly, "Praise the Lord." It was after that when I noticed her mouth was fixed.

On September 18, I experienced problems swallowing again. I said my prayer that the Lord told me to say before eating, however I was still having trouble. I recognized this as again an attack of the Adversary. I panicked and threw my food away. I cannot tell you how awful I felt. I was so ashamed of myself. I felt like I had let God down. The disappointment in myself was so bad, I went downstairs and began praying to God and asking Him for forgiveness. Before long, I was speaking in tongues and crying out loud. I finished by thanking God for His grace and mercy and asked Him to increase my faith and trust in Him.

During the same day as my attack from Satan, my Uncle and Aunt Bishop Roland and First Lady June Hariston were visiting here from Seattle, Washington conducting our yearly family Impartation. Uncle Roland was preparing to write his sermon since he was preaching Sunday morning at our church, and God told him to write a sermon about fear and to use the Book of 2 Timothy Chapter 1, verse 7 as his scripture. When I heard his sermon, I began shouting and rejoicing in the name of Jesus. I asked Uncle Roland when he decided to preach this sermon, and he said it was Saturday evening when God told him what to preach. I told Uncle Roland that it was Saturday evening when I asked God to help me to increase my faith and trust in Him. I praise the name of the Lord. He is always on time. My battles with the Adversary attacking my throat lasted until November 16. I was watching the news and getting dressed for work, when God told me to turn the station to 373 which is The Word network. This network broadcasts religious programs. The minister speaking said you know when you're doing a job for God and you're doing a good job, the devil will attack your throat but no matter if you have to crawl on your hands and knees to get God's job done don't give up and always know that God is right there with you. He then said, "Well, that's all the time I have for today thank you for listening and God bless you." I began rejoicing and praising God. When I went to work, I was able to eat food without any problems. My battle with the Adversary was over. God got the glory and I got the victory. It's important that we continue to give God the glory and thank Him for our healing no matter what.

I knew my battles with Satan were not over, I just didn't

know how he would attack me. I walked around with my antennae up, always keeping a watchful eye for the enemy. Just because things are going smoothly doesn't mean he isn't there. I had finished eight chapters in the Lord's book when all of a sudden our computer developed some type of a problem. Our computer was used for just about everything you could imagine. We had important information stored up as well as the Lord's Book. We asked our cousin Carol to come over and see if she could figure out how to fix whatever was wrong. After several attempts, Carol told us she was unable to correct the problem and suggested we call the man who sold us the computer. Following her suggestion, Larry phoned Larson Scott, from Computer Works. Mr. Scott built our computer for us so he was familiar with the way it functioned. He took our computer and after a couple of days, he phoned us and said our computer had developed some type of virus. We had purchased the most elite type of virus protection there was, but it wasn't enough. Larson told us that all of our documents we had stored had been wiped out by this virus. Everything was gone except the Lord's Book. Mr. Scott stated that it looked like someone was writing a book about God. He informed us that the work on the Lord's Book was the only thing that was saved. When my husband Larry told me this, I told him, "It reminds of the Book of Philippians, Chapter 2, verse 10 and it reads; 'That at the name of Jesus every knee should bow, of things in heaven, and things in earth, and things under the earth.' " Even the virus had to bow down and it was not allowed to penetrate the work of the Lord. I praise the name of Jesus.

The most recent attack on me by Satan occurred on Friday, January 14, 2005. I was attending my Aunt Tee's surprise 65th birthday party. My family, along with 150 family and friends, gathered at a hotel for fun and fellowship. Satan knew that I was just about finished writing the Lord's book and his time was running out. The evening was cold and required people to wear coats. The hotel had only one coat rack displayed for 150 people. I was sitting at a table directly in front of the coat rack. Several guests attending the function asked repeatedly for another coat rack, however the hotel did not respond to our requests.

Around 9:00 P.M., while we were being served our dinner, the coat rack fell on top of me, hitting me in my neck, back, and left arm and pinning me down to the table. It took my husband and four other grown men to pull the coat rack off of me. My cousin grabbed my hand and pulled me out of the chair. I was taken to the hospital and checked out by the emergency room doctor. He ordered X-rays taken of my neck, back, and shoulder and upon him reviewing the pictures, he stated that I was very lucky that my neck wasn't broken or no damage to my spine had occurred. He also said I was lucky that no bones were broken. Luck had nothing to do with it. Again, even the coat rack had to bow before Jesus. What Satan set out to destroy, God turned around for His glory. God allowed the guests to witnesses a miracle taking place right before their eyes. If you stop and think, it took five grown men to get the coat rack off of me and I only had a sprained neck, and arm. I went through physical therapy and expect a full recovery. I thank and praise the name of the Lord for He is worthy of all the praise.

I have been truly blessed by God. In my walk with Him, I have learned many things. I read my Bible every day and pray continuously. There are three particular scriptures that I read each and every day without fail and they are: 2 Corinthians, Chapter 12, verses 7–10, 2 Timothy, Chapter 1, verse 7 and 2 Timothy, Chapter 4, verses 2–5. These scriptures seem to give me the strength and endurance to continue to do the work of the Lord and prepare me for battle with Satan. May the peace of the Lord be with you all.